This Is the
Second Coming

THIS IS THE
SECOND COMING

God's Second Tool

Library of Congress Control Number: 2021910577
ISBN: Hardcover   978-1-6641-0561-4
                 Softcover   978-1-6641-0560-7
                 eBook   978-1-6641-0559-1

Print information available on the last page.

Rev. date: 05/20/2021

To order additional copies of this book, contact:
Xlibris
AU TFN: 1 800 844 927 (Toll Free inside Australia)
AU Local: 0283 108 187 (+61 2 8310 8187 from outside Australia)
www.Xlibris.com.au
Orders@Xlibris.com.au
824018

Chapter 1

So here we are, we are here, a special time in time where the sky is no longer the limit.

These days we've pretty much got time and life under comfortable control.

Power and technology allow us to achieve a comfortable life more comfortably.

So times are good and good times are had. But there is still more to feel bad about than there is to feel good about when all you have to hope for is to shrivel up and die.

Life as we know it is a tragedy

We are the living dead or so the world believes but dosen't even know it

There called decades, you'll only get 3 or 4
and no more than 10 or 12 before your time is
decade and time has decade you

Simply because there's something you've been
missing.

If you found out that you don't have to shrivel
up and die,

How would you handle that

Because that's what I think.

And this Message is simply the BABLE of my
thoughts
and I don't know them to be true.

But if it is imppossible to live without dying

Then it's the end of the world

No one should ever bring another person into
that.

I'm dropping that mystery load.

I hope to take that silent but deadly

K out of this world

Why would knife have a silent but deadly K in front of it.

Probably because you couldn't hear it comming before it killed you

What's the point of life if that's what's gonna kill you

Words are for their meanings (amoung other things)

And they are quite often mean and nasty and mean pain primitive pain, possible pain da inevadable no bullshit extra scrutuating root awaiting

RUDE AWAKENING

All have consequences
that conquer the SEQUENCES
Like unfailing SECURITY

Security is only necessary when there is a potential for danger.

We all gnow life is FRORT with danger

From OURSELVES from EACHOTHER

From NATURE and from GOD

And only an idiot who dosent gnow he's an
idiot would say there is no GOD

Unless he actualy gnows there is no GOD

But if you don't gnow then you have to say
I DON'T GNOW
Or at the very least or the very most
which eva way you want to look at it

You should say what if there could be

"So WHAT IF"

If there is a God,

That would make us the makers property, and
my own life would not belong to me. It may
have come for free. But it turns out I DON'T
OWN MY OWN LIFE

The maker would own me

Hence
We're all living on borrowed
TIME

If you wanna own your own life

You have to make it or pay for it.

The only part of our lives we own

IZ the PAST and PRESENT

Behaviour
You Get to BE, HAVE
and it's all YOURS.

So this begs a question

Has Satan felt the guilt from his behaviour
and thought about REPENT yet
Is that an option for him
How long has it been
How old was he before the FALL

Who am I to say he dosent

Exist

Somewhere in the Bible it says

Woe to you oh earth and sea

For the Devil sends the Beast with Roth

Let him who have understanding wrecken the
number of the Beast

Because he must be NUMB by now

I think this is how that B ended up on the end
of the word numb

Numbers will make you numb

If you want to start counting

Numbers will make you numb untill you get to
the last number

Numbers are evidence of eternity
But that's just me trying to sound sophisticated.
The very fact that I'm here now is evidence of
Eternity

Time is always going to Exist

And so are we, Aparently

Stuck in Eternity with no way out

It's called Captivity

So
I'm Wondering how
the Devils going.

Are we still waiting for him to unleash the beast

I think not

Him and his beast were hear long before we
were
and his beast has done its Damage
And it's all Damed up in the Dam

God had to put him in a cage, because he
turned into a beast

I'm wondering
hasen't he seen enough yet

Isn't his beast getting old tired Buggered and
Ugly

UGLY IZ UGLY
even he dosent like ugly
He must be getting ready to change his
miserable mind.

Who likes being miserable

I'm sure he's aware of what a FOOL he has been

Has it only been 50 million years since the fall

50 million years is much less than a Billion

Testament
Its
meant
ta
test Ya

You got the old testament and the new testament

And this testament
Evoyri days a test
Evoyri word is a test
and before the word comes the thought
Carefull what you think

We are in this for an eternity
You are much better off being crucified than
doing the crucifying in the long run

I think God would have you flogged and
crucified before you ever thought about hurting
another person

We are in this for eternity

I think Satan gnows he is living a lie

A lie that has plagued mankind with confusion.
Confusions reign over man has always been
unfashionable. Unfashionable people don't
often go far in society

So it's been important not to look confused.

I think society the social side of the scene
Has been built on confusion

That's probably why civilization is not a
complete success

Opposites often put us in a position

You gotta negotiate the negative and afarm a positive position that gives us the ability to cultivate a sure Culture.

But if the world continues to be populated with f'n idiots by f'n idiots then were always gonna have f'n idiots to deal with as problems.

It would be hard to stay a virgin all your life, and why would you want to.

But you don't bring other people into a world who are just gonna shrivel up and die.

Life is sexualy transmitted and Lethal (I got told that one by another human)

Evoyri child means another graive grave in the ground

This is UNATURAL and we all think it's natural and normal.

If that's all life has to offer, forget about it, It's a tragedy.
Death is unatural

If you get to heaven and find out you didn't
have to shrivel up and die.

Your gonna be upset by that
dissapointed

You should need a licence and a LIE SENSE and
LIFE SENSE
Before you can have children

(I said that to my pair rents when I was
about 12)
Without the LIE SENSE and LIFE SENSE
Or your children will probably be plagued by
the lie that plagues the world.

If you breed you sign up to be somebodys servant

I would hold pair rents responsible for the
people they produce

Because right now the earth iz an ER with a
thugy TH on the end of it and a big ARE in the
middle.

I think sex is our weakness that makes us weak
when we fall for it

But if you don't fall for it, it becomes your
strength.
If Samson never had a hair cut his hair would
be six metres long by the time he was 30

If it were not a pleasure to fornicate I wonder
if man would still have survived.

I doubt it. So were all pretty much just the result
of something that feels nice

The first men God made Adam and Eve Adam
was At em and Eve was female and something
to do with the night.

Pair rents are not much more than a spurt out
of their daddy's dick.

If there is nothing standing in the way of
nature
It's going to run its course
So the creature
IZ CREATED

We are much more than creatures
untill we get old and creepy

Life as we gnow it iz a tragedy

Breeding iz for the animals

(Because they don't gnow any better)

There is much I'm sure I don't

gnow about LIFE

But I'm sure we have more than

Just 5 Basic Senses

We have 10 that I gnow of

See taste smell touch Listen

Spirituality (Happiness and Saddness)

(The movie is just bullshit)

♥   ♥   ♥

Your Basic Common Sense

Activity

Sexuality

And like the Hate

And somewhere amoungst the like and hate
IZ LOVE

I think even the animals have 10 senses
Even they have the basics, right down to the
crocodile and mabye even the leech

I think only the animals get

Reincarnated

God only made so many animal souls
And they get recycled

Chewbacca wasn't called chewy for no reason.
(Is he just a dog who evolved)

He chewed back time or should I say or should
I say nature, with his simple apreci action
Which is highly appreciated

OR MABYE he simply had a good Master

(Who Had WITH) AUTHORITY

to bring out the best in him

And this is simply to result of Nature

(The word authority realy just means)

HELPING TO GROW

And don't be surprised by the SIR PRIZE

It's Nature
MATTER
And with unlimited GEOLOGICAL
Cappabilities that nature
IZ LIMITED BY

It's going to take time and dedication

PRECIOUS PRESSURE and TIME

PRECIOUS TIME

I think our makers name IZ ZION (that's sigh
on with a ZZZ)

Is iron the most precious metal in the world.
If there is any one element that has made
man's plight progress

IT IZ IRON

Rasputin, that's what I think ZION calls the
devil (who do evil) live spelt backwards
Living the wrong way

He's always disputin the dis put IN

that he put IN

After the fall
ZION says to Rasputin
Come back to me
If you will serve me as a friend.
That's why I made YOU

And just think, if you made a

beautiful man to spend your time with (women
are men to)

You would be horrified if they turned against
you. You would get no pleasure in destroying
them

Unless you actualy made them to fight with.

So the maker just wants to be friends.
Because he's got this huge problem.

Called Eternity

And needs some company of a pleasant person
to help

beat the burden of Eternity.

But Rasputin still upset refused

and promised he will always refuse

So Zion called him by a different Name.
With much pain and anguish

(He realy struggled to say this I think)

Or shortened Breath
TURNING AWAY
He called him Satan
Bearly finishing the word.
That was after politely calling him aloof.
A goofy loof.
50 million years later Rasputin finds out.
Zion realy called him Say TURN

and look behind you

50 million years is much less than a billion.

I think he must be ready to change his misserable mind.

And admit defeat

Who likes being misserable.

Why are we here.
I think simply to enjoy it
What's the point of life if you can't enjoy it.

Oh and God's got this huge problem called Eternity
And needs some friends to beat the burden of Eternity

There will come a time when men simply choose pleasure over pain

And gnowing what emoats pleasure and

What emoats pain would make it near effortless I would imagine.

A man can only truly be free when

he gnow's he is free from his own

demize and death
Freedom is pleasure

But freedom dosent come for free.

You pay for your death with your ignorance.
And if you want to keep your Life
You have to constantly pay for it

It is said that Eternal Vigilance is the price of
freedom.

I would certainly have to agree with that
You gotta pray all day

You can't say your prayers and then switch off

Evoyri thing you do include God

This is God's address this is where you will find
him/her
(It's a God it can take on any form it wants)

I think heaven is on the other side of the sun
And the planets help balance the Solar System

Infamy is in for me

Our maker says if you show for me

I will chaufer you

But you can't open a heart with

a sledge hammer
Oh you could but it would certainly
Break it

There is no limit to how long you can live as a
human

Who am I to say otherwise

IZ IZ WHAT IF's Gonna be

That's the new future IZ and IF

Meet you optimist it IZ IF

But IF can also be your pesty pessimist

Depending on your attitude and where

Your TUDE IZ AT

A little fort around your TUDE will give you
FORTITUDE

A TUDE with a nice TUNE and a

FUTURE without FOO IN YOU

So be carefull what you chew on

You are what you eat

E goes with E and E goes with go

E's nasty meaning iz go, and where

you get to go goes with you and

depends on you to get you where your going.
Come and see the minds eye

Not transfixed upon the why

Just the E
Make the E that goes go strong
Without your ego

Those faultless Vocal Vowels Contain an
Eternal Potential Hey

E I O U What you made me for

Go and do are often the same

What you do in your minds eye

Creates your destiny
I think JEDI would mean straight eye
A minds eye eternaly vigilant on his
maker
and his makers REQUIRMENTS

Oh
And the Holy Grail
It IZ A

GREY ILL and it's holy

To drink from the same cup

Jesus was given

To serve only good when bad

Is served to you

And to maintain a little fort around Your
TUDE
This iz what it takes to be a fool for the HOLY
GREY ILL

And as for LOVE

I've been told by another Human, that LOVE
Stands for Legs Open Very Easy
But that's not what LOVE IZ
There is a reason Love hurts
You have like and hate
What do you need Love for

Love is sacrifice
Or as I like to say
The bullshit you put up with when things start
going wrong with a relationship you like.
(Amoung other things)

And as for religion.
Religion just means you gotta go do this and
you gotta go

do that, but these acts don't acheive much if
anything at all.

I don't think religion comes from God

Because there are so many to choose from
Religion is man's IDEA

God does not make Catholics or Muslims etc

People try to make these things
Religion is for people who can't think
For themselves
If there were such a thing as religion
Evoyri one would gnow about it.
IZ there a single religious person out there
Who actualy gnows this is what you must do

Evoyri religous person does so because

their clueless. The only thing you will find at church
IZ a whole lot of other clueless people
Who are looking for GOD

There are no religions
JUST BEHAVIOUR
I'm sorry
If this upsets you

You may have just found yourself

in the wrong. Nobody likes to be

found IN THE WRONG.

I've seen a lot of trouble in my time and I gnow
I don't want to see anymore

I think there may come a time when there IZ
Only one jail left in the world
And it will be a church
That's all church iz good for (Hosier)

And as for Marriage
While your waiting for someone to tell you, you
are now married

As you vow for better or for worse till death due
us part
Don't forget to say or untill we feel the need for
a devorce
Do you think you are now married because he
says so
I wanna sue the bloke who married my pair
rents, because he wasn't qualified to marry
anyone
The only time your married is when your
intercourse
ING
You can never make another person YOURS

(As much as you'd like too)

Three lies in this world

Death
Marriage
Religion

But if you want to get married

YOU CAN TRY

So good luck with your lives

It's your choice and you have no

choice but to choose
And if what I think and say
Iz not true
You'll have wasted your life being the most
pleasant
person you can be

And as for the Gay Issue

God must make people who are

GAY, who am I to say otherwise

But remember
Sex is your weakness
(So I Believe)
There is no limit to how
Long you can
LIVE
Who am I to say otherwise

Somewhere it is written in the Bible
Broad is the road to Death and destruction
Narrow is the road to everlasting LIFE
But in this day and age I would turn that
around.
Narrow is the road to death and destruction,
Broad iz the road to everlasting LIFE

The path to God may have many Lanes on
many Levels
There may be infinite lanes and levels

To be anywhere near God's level

I think you would have to think past a hundred
years.
Start thinking forever people
That's WHAT YOU HAVE

IN FRONT OF YOU
I think this is what it iz TO BE
BORN AGAIN

There iz no escaping this CAPTIVITY

50 Billion years iz an ever shrinking spec
as eternity be and Leaves it behind

But a plumb will help level you

Believe is just another word for think
What are you gonna Be and what are You
gonna Leave

And as for war
If you couldn't find anyone to fight a war
you'd never have another war again

Soldier - Sold your soul to who Soldiers take
orders and do what their told

Back in the old days to help organize a young
soldier

A dead enemy soldier's rib cage would be cut
open, and the chest plate removed

So they could Organ Eyes their young Soldiers

They used to be able to shock a lot

With chocholate
Only the shock was such a pleasure

I think people need to find something

to make life harder for themselves

to find some happiness in an accomplishment.

It IZ VERY IMPORTANT THAT THAT THING YOU
FIND TO MAKE LIFE HARDER FOR YOURSELF

BE GOOD FOR YOU AND MAKE YOU STRONGER

Don't start liking something

that is bad for YOU
The seconds are called this because you couldn't
call them firsts or thirds the minutes are mini
and minute the hours are usually our ERS the
week's are something to do with being weak I
find the morning quite sad and somber a drop
is not a drip until it drops and a spurt is just a

drip under pressure a scene is not a seen until
it's been looked at

There's a meaning there but the meaning there
dosen't realy mean a

Thing

Come and see the real Thing
Come and see the real Thing
Come and see

I am the real thing

And I can hardly believe it
MYSELF

You would never expect it to be

IN YOUR WILDEST DREAMS

And I am a BIG

DREAMER

The months are something to do with mountains
Amounting

And the Years they rhym with Tears

And the tier indicates different Levels (of Saddness)

Nobody likes saddness

Life is inevatibly sad when your only gonna

Shrivel up and die

Those old people have been raped

of evoyri thing that's good about

THEM

This may be the Second Comming

the world has been waiting for, for all I gnow.

Yeh that's right
I think I God Second Son

But I DON'T GNOW THAT I AM

And you don't gnow I'm not

But regardless of who I am

OR who I'm not

People need to start thinking for real

Your in this mess

and your gonna find it harder and harder till

you simply can't go on (Probably)

This is pathetic

to welcome your children into the living dead

We have a mean God

Who means to GET WHAT HE WANTS

If you gnew how to live without dying

(Technology) anyone could do it

The REAL BEAUTY LY's in

NOT GNOWING

Because if you don't gnow and still

accomplish a life worthy of not DYING

Now that's an impressive rare DIAMOND

With some geo logic pressure

and time

You can be a DIAMOND

What God IZ God to us

If he can't save us from Death

What Good iz life to us

If we can't save ourselves

From death.

Chapter 2

This is what makes me think I am God's second Son

I HAVE BEEN TOLD
Loud and clear, but in a round about way

By SOMEONE WHO IZ DEAD

But I can't say he's dead because

HE SPOKE TO ME

I was out to do some shopping, just hoped on a train, and thought to myself, why am I the only one who gnows all this stuff

Then my old friend who's now passed on told me "YOUR GOD'S TOOL" as in God's second son.

That's what DAWNED ON ME as I was told "YOUR GOD'S TOOL."

It was February 4 2009 2 days before my 37th birthday

Fair to say I got the shock of my LIFE

Just for a second or two
MY JAW HIT THE GROUND (so to speak)

Then I had to go do the shopping

So at the very least

I GNOW I'M GOD'S TOOL

This is what makes me think you can LIVE without DYING.

Somewhere in the later part of the year 2000
I had a faint whisper
And it said
"JESUS IZ THE ONLY MAN BORN TO DIE."

It was just a tiny whisper

Soon after that I found a new word for death

I'VE FOUND A NEW WORD FOR DEATH =
UNATURAL

Soon after that I found 4 extra senses

At the age of 21 or 22 I had this strange
YOUR GONNA BE FAMOUS
ITS GONNA BE YOU AND THE WORLD

That one was like a thought, but why would I
ever think I'm gonna be Famous.
And just after that I had a strong sensation of
someone looking down on me

Infamy is in for me, but I think it best if I
remain annonamous

Somewhere in my late teens 17 or 18

I HAD MY HEART SPEAK TO ME

WITH WORDS THAT I HEARD

BUT NOT WITH MY EARS

Let me go into detail

Something that I can only describe

as a feeling, I felt in the left

hand side of my chest right where

my HEART BEATS
It lasted no more than a second or two,
I don't want to go into what it said
That's irrelivant
But I must say, it didn't have anything
GOOD to say
But it did FEEL GOOD
It spoke the same way I DO

It was like their way somebody else inside me

I DIDN'T GNOW ABOUT

It wasn't till about 3 weeks later
I was thinking about what that was

And Hey
THAT WAS GOD
I think you could call it a TOTAL ECLIPSE OF
THE HEART
It was an extrordinary Feeling

At the age of 26, I met someone for the first time

and in pops my head

YOUR A NARELLAN BOY IF I'VE EVER SEEN ONE

Six months later I find out he's a Narellan boy
Raised in Narrellan

So I've had a few voices tell me things.
First one was in my heart

The rest have been in my Head

The last one "YOUR GOD'S TOOL"

Was loud and clear
and I recognized who was talking to me

OFTEN I can't believe it myself
You think your God's second son

You would never expect it to be in Your wildest
dreams.
But take a step back for a little while and find
it their.
It's something I find hard to explain.
But I remain trapped inside my lonely life

Lonelyness It's my place.

And this is an S.O.S. to the world

It's all been prophesized and continues to be
prophesized by the prophets

Who profit from their propheses

They Will Prophecy

What are these people singing about

When did the FINAL COUNT DOWN begin

WELCOME TO THE NEW AGE
THIS IZ IT THE APPOCOLYPSE

(That's the Oh pucker lips)

It's all over the radio

It's the end of the world as we

GNOW IT

Death iz not a when it's an IF

And if your thinking of killing someone

DON'T THINK THEY CAN'T COME BACK

The only sure thing in LIFE

IZ TAXES

Do you see what I see

I can go on and on about all these songs that
ring a bell in my head.

There's probably 1000 songs I could name
as propheses about ME and this THIS

And there's probably 1000's I'm not aware
of yet.

I am not in this by meself

I'm an Idiot, but never mind that

BLOW THE WHISTLE

YOUR THE REFEREE

I'm hoping to get it down like New York City

I think it's the end of the world not because
were all dying.

But simply because the house iz FULL

The world can only feed so many people

Over population iz becoming quite a big Issue.
The world iz not unlimited by the amount of
people it can house and feed

Nor do I think Heaven iz unlimited by the
amount of people it can HOUSE

As big as it IZ
Stretching from here to pluto on the other side
of the SUN (so I think)

It IZ NOT UNLIMITED (so I Believe)

We gnow it's been quite a few

thousand years of humanity, and if

it's been millions.
Heaven must be very FULL

Reaching numbers that are to big for Humans

But there is no limit to how long You can live
as a human (so I believe)

(Immortle status just may be possible)

Just give him (God) what he wants

Always do the best you can do

And I've gotta find some more BABLE

to RAMBLE on with so a book Publisher will
bother Publishng this Message
FOR
THE
MESS
AGE

We all live in
Even God couldn't tell you what the next lotto
numbers are gonna be (awe I'm pretty sure
about that) but you gotta be in it to win it
there's no hope of winning without a ticket
We all need to win lotto or just the ones who
have to eat when their told if you want to
make a major improvement in this world you
can not only allow some poor person to eat at
a certain particular time and for how long
weather their ready or not Human beings
are high maintenance active people require
constant fueling so their energy needs are met

constantly and comfortably only allowing some poor person to eat at a certain particular time and for how long weather their ready or not iz a crime and a sure way to slowly kill them if you dont get what you need you will die dying people are not happy the humanization of the poulation iz my aim often we are treated like machines People children need to be able to take care of themselves Placing such ridiculous restrictions on people is a crime DEATH IS AVOIDABLE and your gonna need your health to beat DEATH

And many food companies would be under some serious scrutiny you can t feed this stuff to a population and expect a healthy populas UNHEALTHY PEOPLE ARE NOT happy many lived much better lives 2000 years ago All they would eat is meat and vegetables and bread for SUGAR IT IS NOT common gnowledge to PEOPLE that sugar is ACID TO MUCH ACID BURNS YOUR BODY DIABETES it's a case of the DIRES and you got all this acid BEATING on the walls of your arteries and every where else the blood goes

Welcome to the New Age
THIS IZ IT THE APPOCOLYPSE

I am the Appocolypse,

And I'm just another fool in the crowd

Born and raised by a pair of f'n idiots. (quite common)

I was born in a cross fire hurricane (quite common)

Raised by a toothless bearded Head (quite common)

My muddled mother keeps spreading her legs for someone she hates (quite common)

I believe she said to God

"DON'T GIVE ME HIS" SON"

"GIVE ME YOUR SON"

(That's not that common)

And Hence

They and the world

GOT ME

It's been to many years since I

found out (or got told) who I am

I nearly 12 now

Adel singing we could have had

IT ALL

But I played it to the beat

Throw my soul through every open door

Turn his sorrow into treasured Gold

OR he's gonna make my Head

BURN

I think God just might put me on a planet all
by myself if I don't give him what he wants

We all have the power off God Within us
I think you'll find it in Grace

That Amazing Grace

I don't think he will lend you his power without
that

Seek ye first the kingdom of God

And His rightousness, and all these

Things shall be added unto you

AH AH AH are ALLELUIA

ALLELUIA AH AH AH are ALLELUIA

AH LEIGH LOU YA

AH are are are ALLELU ALLELUIA

Sing ALLELUIA

So I'm feeling kind of desperate

desperation

Evoyri one iz in the FIGHT OF THEIR LIFE

Including me

I believe in a better way

With the world the way it iz

People are expected to work fast and

dy Young (100 years iz Young)

It's a human race and if you can't keep up
you'll get left behind

One thing I gnow about life

It's MEAN

To help make it Less Mean

I would opt for, One day on

One day off. So we don't kill

ourselves.
Especially if your doing big days

Especially if the heat of summer

Many spend way to much time at work

Being a human being iz work

IN ITSELF

I can Sum Life up as three

Things

Diet

Relationships

Exercise
Not allowing someone to work- more tha one
day on one day off.

May be a crime in a human race

But I think it would be a necesity
When your faced with more than a hundred
years

Then we would only spend half of our lives at
work

There would be more work to go around
Less unemployment

More time for Relationships, Diet and Exercise
Being a human being

IZ WORK IN ITSELF

You have to give people time to be people

We are not machines

This may help people have time to enjoy

their lives, what's the point of life if

You can't enjoy it.

Times now may be good and good

times had but they could be better

There are to many angry people out there

Angry people are not happy

This transition won't happen over night

It may take a hundred years to be implemented

But it's a necesity if you want to

live in a happy world with much less crime
This crime I would like to implement may
totaly eliminate crime

Only unhappy people commit crimes

You got your left hand your right hand

and if you don't take what's right you'll

only have what's Left.

And the left can't live without the Right.
So I believe this would be the Right thing to do

Oh
And it is never alright to hit your children
Under any circumstances

The only thing that allows you to hit

Your little children is the fact that you are
bigger, and stronger than they are

Using such Vile behaviour is Thugish

Using such Thugish behaviour is Vile

It's a rude world we live in
When evoyri pair rent thinks it
OK for their children to shrivel up and die

You are always going to be some silly person
who thinks it's alright for them to shrivel up
a die.

Do not expect your children to be like you
Do not expect them to be happy with you
Expect them to Depend on you

You are their servant

If you want to live in a perfect world
You simply can't allow just any fuckhead
to have children

It's as simple as that

Nobody wants a mum who don't gnow how to
live without dying

If you don't gnow how to live without dying
It's unlikely your gonna do what's required

We are all just here to amuse God
If you took away the earth

that would be like taking away God's T.V.
So I believe

I'm sorry if I gnow to much

Nobody likes a gnow it all

But I don't gnow what I gnow

And I gnow I don't gnow

I'm just some poor person who's

heard the sound of the strangest voices
Hence I believe I'm the GREAT SOUTHERN LAND

This concept is living without dying is
nothing new.

It's in the first few pages of the Bible
Somebody goes to heaven without dying

So thy kingdom come
and I'm the dumb king
and guess what
Your a King or Queen
We are all Kings or Queens of ourselves
(once)
(When) We can think for ourselves

And make decisions from the choices we choose

A let me say, I've lost my religion
I hope I've said enough
I hope I haven't said too much

Just give me what I gnow IZ MINE
Here's to the future, Hear the cry of YOUTH

But I don't want it all

I only want what pleases me

So PEACE to all who enter here the peice of life
evoyri one would choose and hope for I hope

All these wars are over

To Christ the cross (Lord have mercy)

And to me the chair

Now we won't be raped (Hopefully)

Now we won't be scared like that

Forgiveness it's a necesity

We are in this for eternity
You can die but your never dead
You can't bring your wars into God's House

You will break his chandeliers

There's been war in heaven once but it was
quickly stamped out

It's important to be and remain a

fool for the Holy Grey ILL

if you get happy about war

You will loose your Halo

So lay low don't get happy about

Something like that, suffer the pain

This is why Love Hurts

If you play a walk on part in a war

You may play a lead role in a cage

I think God will tell you

If war is what you want

You can have it, But not here

You'll break my chandeliers

It will be in a cold dimly lit place
Up the back of heaven

In the demonic Realm.

Heaven has Real Estate much like the Earth

Dangerous people are not destined for

fine sought after real estate in Heaven

It's important to be and remain

Harmless

And God has gone to extreme Lengths
to try and make some serious Sinners
Feel Sorry.

To save them from Homelessness

Evoyri one has their own personal

Jesus, and what does yours look like

Sorrow iz the only good that can

Come out of sin
Sorrow iz sorry Sorrow (not pleasure)

Sin may sign you up for eternal sorrow

PAIN, not happiness

Sorrow is embarrising

Mabye well have a better understand-
ING to stand under

Welcome to Eternity

But I would not welcome somebody else into
this never ending story

Or you'll find yourself praying

I Think you will find there's not a

single person who has lived who did

not feel the need to pray at some point

In their life
He is the God of you and you will need to make him
feel like it

And I would urge evoyri one

to pray, for that poor old Lucifer

I remember saying back when I was about 21 yrs old

"Even the Devil will repent

God made him

If it's been 50 million yrs since his fall he's probably got 50 million years of reperation in front of him

He's probably gonna need some help

And maybe we can eliminate a

Great Evil that has plagued our

Eternal Universe for so Long

Even he would not accept the

Behavior he try's to give

I think the time iz comming

Sooner Rather than later

He will admit defeat.

And I hear from people who are

IN THE GNOW

THAT OUR HOUSE IZ IN SERIOUS

DANGER

And that we need to act now and act FAST

I think this world has got big problems comming

But if we don't act now and act fast
It's going to be rather catastrophic

And I would STRONGLY suggest

that NOBODY BRING ANYBODY ELSE

INTO THIS FULL HOUSE We have conquered this world (somewhat)

All that iz left to conquer

IZ DEATH